FAMILY WALKS
IN SOUTH
SHROPSHIRE
AND THE
WELSH BORDERS

Marian Newton

Scarthin Books, Cromford, Derbyshire   1993

FAMILY WALKS
IN SOUTH SHROPSHIRE
AND THE WELSH BORDERS

Family Walks Series
General Editor: Norman Taylor

THE COUNTRY CODE

Guard against all risk of fire
Fasten all gates
Keep dogs under proper control
Keep to paths across farm land
Avoid damaging fences, hedges and walls
Leave no litter
Safeguard water supplies
Protect wildlife, wild plants and trees
Go carefully along country roads
Respect the life of the countryside

Phototypesetting, printing by Black Bear Press Limited,
Cambridge, England

ISBN 0 907758 30 4

CLUN CASTLE

For my husband Graham and our friends Betty and Colin
who have shared many happy walks.

Preface

On one of our earliest family walks in Shropshire we led our two
young daughters on a 7 mile afternoon trek without any refreshment or
tea breaks. We had just acquired our first walking book obviously written
for seasoned ramblers and we struggled on through torrential rain and
deep mud without any thought of surrender. I think the only 'attraction'
on the walk was an enormous horse chestnut tree with lots of conkers
which weighted us down on the return journey. At tea time we were lost
and very confused because the Forestry Commission had felled a large
area of woodland and it was with great relief we finally found the right
track. I was beginning to think we would have to sleep under the stars!

This walking book is especially for families — I hope it will introduce
you to a beautiful part of Britain and help you avoid the mistakes we first
made as family walkers. If you move to a new area a walking book is a
wonderful way to get to know the countryside. Our first book is now a
treasured possession — it gave us a real love for the border countryside
with its rolling hills and quiet villages.

I would like to thank my family for their help and encouragement
and for their special contributions — my daughter Juliet for all the
illustrations, my husband Graham and my father for the photographs,
and my daughter Caroline for providing delicious meals on our return.
This really is a family walking book! I am very grateful to my husband for
all his planning and navigating and for persuading me to buy my first pair
of walking boots!

About the author

Marian Newton has lived in Shropshire for 18 years. She is married
to a farm manager and teaches at Corvedale School near Ludlow.

CONTENTS

Map of the area

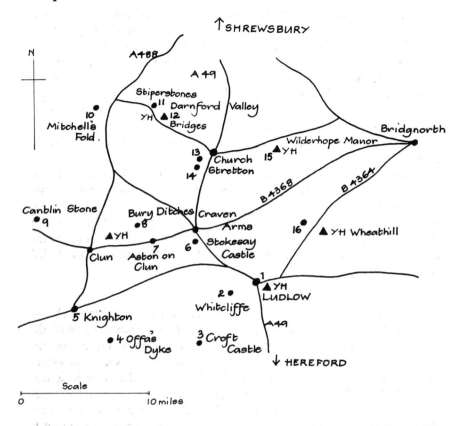

Introduction

The Shropshire countryside that inspired Housman to write of 'those blue remembered hills' is still some of the loveliest in England. It's a land of contrasts with rugged hills and high lonely moorland, rolling farmland and evergreen forests, peaceful hamlets and bustling market towns. The border conflict has left a fine legacy of castles and the borderlands are rich with tales and folklore. There is so much to enjoy in this region — the variety of landscape, the ancient buildings and the wonderful quality of quiet, rural life.

This book is intended to help families explore the border countryside. The routes are planned with the interests and stamina of children in mind and tend to be comparatively short with a refreshment stop en route. Road walking has been kept to a minimum and on many walks the most strenuous part is tackled first. The walks are circular and vary between 1½ and 7 miles. Under the heading 'Attractions' there is mention of the special features which may appeal to children and parents too! — such as streams and waterfalls, castles and legends, unusual birds and flowers.

Choosing a walk

Unless the children are seasoned walkers it is advisable to choose one or two of the easier walks first. Try not to be too ambitious. With the very young children, the 3 to 6 year olds, start by walking interesting parts of the routes and always be prepared to turn back. Sometimes just a walk along a stream is enough as in the Darnford Valley and Knighton walks. If the children enjoy their first expeditions they will look forward to a family walk. Why not share a walk with another family or let the children bring a young friend? Chatting with their friends they forget to notice the passage of time and their tired legs!

Some 5 year olds accustomed to country walks can manage a 4 mile trek. An 8 year old doing it for the first time may find the same walk too strenuous. Start with the shorter easier walks and build up gradually to the difficult ones. At the back of the book you will find a list of the routes in order of difficulty.

Allowing sufficient time

Each walk is intended as the best part of a days outing allowing time for play, exploration and rest stops. It is better to over-estimate rather than underestimate the time it may take. As a rough guide allow a pace of around a mile per hour for very young childen graduating to 2 miles per hour for an experienced 11 year old.

What to wear

Weather conditions can change during a day especially on the hills so be prepared. Wet clothes can spoil a day and you may have to abandon your expedition. Equip the family with some lightweight waterproof clothing which can be carried in the rucksacks.

Cagoules are easier for children to pull on and leggings will keep them completely dry in a heavy downpour. Several light layers of clothing are warmer and more comfortable than heavy jackets. Make sure the first layer is a short sleeved shirt or T shirt in case the day is very warm, and include an extra sweater.

Comfortable footwear is essential on family walks. Although proper walking boots are the ideal they are expensive and young children soon grow out of them. Sturdy trainer type shoes are a good substitute with wellingtons for wet, muddy walks. Don't forget warm hats and mittens in winter.

SOPHY AND RHYS USE RUCKSACKS FOR SCHOOL

Rucksacks

Walking with families always involves carrying food and drink and extra clothing but don't let Dad stagger along with a heavy rucksack! Share the load and it can be fun for all the family. Bright inexpensive rucksacks are sold in all sizes so equip everyone with their own rucksack and make them responsible for en route refreshments and storm gear.

Parents can help carry the main picnic and extra clothing. Let the children choose some individual packets of fruit juice and high energy food, and have some extra breaks on the walk to enjoy these.

Children will find walks more interesting if they can identify some of the birds and flowers seen on the expedition. They can carry their own lightweight spotter books and refreshment stops are a good opportunity to make positive identification. If the children have their own rucksacks then they are responsible for anything collected en route i.e. conkers, pebbles. Include a few polythene bags if you are walking in late summer for blackberries and mushrooms. Flower specimens will travel home in a small polythene bag if you blow in some air and secure the opening. A most important item for the adult rucksack is a small first aid kit for cuts and grazes.

Public rights of way

All the walks in this guide follow public rights of way. However on parts of several routes due to infrequent use there is little trace of the path. In some cases the right of way may lead straight across a cultivated field. Rather than incur the farmer's wrath walk round the inner edge of the field and regain the footpath.

The maps

The maps in this guide in combination with the route descriptions are sufficiently detailed to be used without reference to any other maps of the area. However there is much enjoyment to be gained from using Ordnance Survey Maps. Why not take the opportunity to teach the children map reading skills and take the local Pathfinder map and a small compass?

Refreshments

Food is a very important part of family walks! It is worthwhile to plan the food and drink needed on the expedition and to decide where the family are going to picnic or eat a meal. These walks are in wild border country — don't be disheartened if there is not a café or inn en route — picnics are great fun and inexpensive.

The most important rule is to take plenty of fruit juice. Let the children carry a little of their own and make sure the adults have extra supplies and some in the car for the end of the walk. Individual cartons of fruit juice are light to carry or there are special water bottles for walkers. Involve the family in planning the picnic — this will add to their anticipation and enjoyment of the day. Aim for food that will travel easily and is refreshing. Soft baps with different fillings, individual quiches, pasties, crunchy salads, gingerbread, flapjack and apples are just a few ideas. Pack the food in lightweight sandwich boxes which protect it from damage on the walk.

Family walks are not just for summer — they can be great fun in cold weather. Soup in a large thermos flask is very warming on a cold day. Making your own drink can be fun too — there are several backpacking stoves on the market which are light enough to carry on a family expedition and these can be used with chocolate drink sachets which take up very little room in a rucksack. The walks will be more enjoyable if you allow some extra breaks for rest and refreshment. Young children get very thirsty and little legs get tired.

Most of the pubs mentioned allow children accompanied by adults into their premises and many have gardens with picnic tables and a play area. Bar meals can be difficult with very young children. Until they are old enough to enjoy a meal why not try a compromise — stopping in a pub garden for refreshing drinks and then returning to the countryside for a picnic. Don't eat your own food on the premises and upset the landlord! If you do plan to buy a meal, remember catering often stops well before closing time.

One final thought for the return home. Everyone will be tired and adults and older children may be ready for a meal. Make sure you have some easily prepared food available or use an automatic timer to have a supper dish cooking in the oven. This makes a happy end to the perfect day!

NORMAN CHAPEL IN LUDLOW
CASTLE

LUDLOW CASTLE

Shrewsbury Biscuits

4 oz butter
4 oz caster sugar
1 egg beaten
8 oz plain flour
2 teaspoons grated lemon rind

Grease 2 baking trays.

Cream the butter and sugar until pale and fluffy. Add the egg a little at a time, beating after each addition. Stir in the flour and lemon rind and mix to a fairly firm dough. Knead lightly and roll out $\frac{1}{8}-\frac{1}{4}$ inch thick on a floured board. Cut into rounds with a $2\frac{1}{2}$ inch fluted cutter and put on the trays.

Bake at 350°F 180°C, Gas Mark 4 for 15–20 mins. until firm and very lightly browned. (If the dough is very soft and difficult to handle, wrap in cling film and leave in a cool place before rolling out.)

Symbols used on the route maps

1	— → — — → —	Route
2	. . . .	Other footpaths **not** en route
3.	════════════	Road
4.	= = = = = = = ==	Track
5.	〰〰〰↗	River or Stream
6	├─┼─┼─┼─┤	Railway
7.	𝕊𝕊 𝕊𝕊 𝕊𝕊	Woods
8		Village
9.	▪	Building
10	✛	Church
11	②	Number corresponds with route description
12	🌲 🌲 🌲 🌲 🌲	Plantation

Ludlow Castle and the River Teme

Outline   Whitcliffe Common ~ River Teme ~ Ludford Bridge ~ Broad Street ~ Ludlow Castle ~ Castle Walk ~ Dinham Bridge ~ Whitcliffe.

Summary   Ludlow has so much to offer family walkers. There is a riverside walk past weirs and over ancient bridges — a medieval town and Norman castle to explore — an adventure playground, putting and rowing — and a beautiful picnic area on Whitcliffe Common with a panorama of hills, church and castle.

Attractions   The riverside path is called the Bread Walk and goes past a quarry of Silurian Limestone. Can the children find the old stone near the steps which marks the level of the great flood of 1888? Watch the water rushing over the long weir.

There are many delightful places for refreshment but the Charlton Arms near Ludford Bridge has picnic tables overlooking the river and picturesque De Grey's Café in Broad Street serves home-made Chelsea buns. Vegetarian food can be found at the Olive Branch Restaurant in the Bullring.

Ludlow Castle is the perfect story-book castle with its great Norman keep and ancient walls. It was begun in 1086 by Roger Lacy as one of the frontier castles between England and Wales and the early years were a time of bloodshed and violence. Later it became a royal castle and the headquarters of the Council of the Marches. Edward IV sent his sons here — the two little princes who were later murdered in the Tower. Climb to the top of the keep and see how the castle commands the surrounding countryside. How far away could you see an enemy army coming?

The Normans created a 'new town' beside the castle with a regular layout of roads in a grid pattern and in 13th century a wall was built around the town. Notice the portcullis slits as you walk through Broadgate — the only survivor of Ludlow's seven gates.

Ludlow is a fascinating town to explore with its half timbered buildings, quaint courtyards and cobbles. In Broad Street, fine Georgian houses lead up to the Buttercross. Look out for the old stocks in Castle Square and then take your seat in the Castle Gardens and enjoy a large ice cream from the Buttery. A cannon captured at the Battle of Sebastopol guards the castle entrance.

The Castle is open 7 days a week from May to September 10.30
continued on page 14

11

Route 1

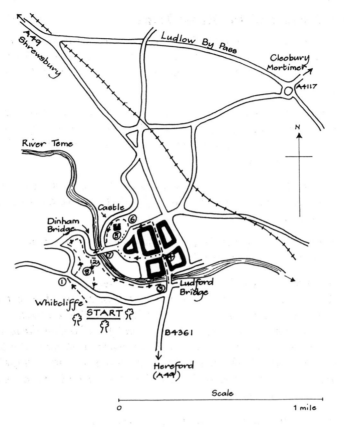

Route 1

Ludlow Castle and the River Teme $2\frac{1}{2}$ miles

START   *Whitcliffe Common, Ludlow. At Ludford Bridge turn off the B4361 on to a minor road signposted Wigmore and Burrington. Excellent car park in $\frac{1}{2}$ mile on the left in a wooded area. GR 505743.*

ROUTE

1. *Walk down the track to the Bowling Green Restaurant. Cross the road on to the Common, turn left and follow the path slightly downhill. Before the path joins the road turn right on to a wide track which curves downhill through the trees to the river.*

2. *At Dinham Bridge turn right and follow the wide path along the river bank. It passes the weir and gradually climbs above the river until it descends a small flight of steps to the road.*

3. *Turn left, cross Ludford Bridge and proceed straight ahead up Lower Broad Street and under the Broadgate.*

4. *There are now 2 possible routes to the Castle:*
   (a) A walk via the Buttercross and Castle Street passing restaurants and inns. Go straight ahead and turn left at the Buttercross.
   (b) A quieter walk by the town wall. Turn left and follow the town wall round, crossing Mill Street. Continue along the wall and take the first turning right into Dinham, climbing uphill past the little chapel of St. Thomas on your left. Cross the road into the Castle Gardens and turn right to the main entrance.

5. *Ludlow Castle. Castle Gardens. Refreshments.*

6. *Follow the Castle Walk to the right of the castle entrance. This curves round the castle walls and then take the second turning on the right down the slope to the swimming pool. Turn right for the recreation ground.*

7. *Cross Dinham Bridge and take the middle path on the left which climbs gradually up the broad Donkey Steps to the Common. Ignore a turning on the right.*

8. *Follow the track to the top, turn right through the trees and cross the road to the parking area.*

ACCESS BY BUS
  To Ludlow from Shrewsbury and Hereford.

a.m.–6 p.m. From October to April it is open from 10.30 a.m.–4 p.m. and closed on Sundays. During the last week in June and the first week in July the Castle is used for the Ludlow Festival and Shakespeare plays are performed in the Inner Bailey.

The castle walk leads down to the recreation ground which is an ideal place for a picnic. There are swings, an adventure playground and a little putting course beside the river. Rowing boats can be hired for a trip on the Teme — a chance to observe ducks and moorhens in their habitat. Enjoy a teatime picnic and a welcome rest on Whitcliffe Common above the town. A small wildflower spotter book would help children to identify the meadow flowers. The woodland shelters many birds including chiffchaffs, nuthatches, long-tailed tits and coal tits and in Summer swifts fly high above the castle.

The poet A. E. Housman captured the spirit of Ludlow

> Oh come you home on Sunday
> When Ludlow's streets are still
> And Ludlow's bells are calling
> To farm and lane and mill.

A Shropshire Lad

Refreshments   The Charlton Arms, Ludlow.   The Cliff, Ludlow.

VIEW FROM CLIMBING JACK COMMON

Route 2   3½ miles
Mary Knoll Forest Trail

Outline   The Vinnals Car Park ~ Sunny Dingle Wood ~ Mary Knoll Valley ~ Climbing Jack Common ~ The Vinnals Car Park and Picnic Area.

Summary   This is a well marked forest trail starting with a valley walk through oakwoods and then a gentle climb to open walking on Climbing Jack Common with magnificent views over the border country.

Attractions   These ancient woodlands were part of the Saxon hunting forest given to Ralph de Mortimer who fought with William at the Battle of Hastings. They are now owned by the Forestry Commission who have laid out waymarked walks from the 2 car parks. There are several short trails suitable for young children who will have fun finding their way by following the colour coded posts. The Mary Knoll walk is a short trail with a variety of scenery through oakwoods and conifer forests and a scramble up Climbing Jack Common which is a carpet of bluebells in May.

The main attraction of Mortimer forest is a large herd of fallow deer. The deer are very sensitive to sound and smell but if the family trek quietly through the woods they may be rewarded by sighting a small group crossing the trail.

The forest is rich in wildlife. In Mary Knoll valley there are nesting boxes on the trees for various species of birds. Spotted woodpeckers loop through the trees and buzzards glide overhead. In late summer watch out for butterflies on the thistles and brambles especially the comma and silver washed fritillary.

The area is famous for its geology — some of the rocks in the forest date from Silurian times, about 400 million years ago. It was once covered by a sub tropical sea and many fine fossil specimens have been collected. Older children will enjoy a visit to the little museum in Ludlow to see these local fossils.

From Climbing Jack Common there are spectacular views of the Clee Hills, the Long Mynd and the Malvern Hills. Legend has it that the children of the Earl of Bridgwater were lost in Mary Knoll valley in 1634 but your family will be quite safe following the brightly marked forest trail! (Illustrated leaflets may be obtained from the Forest District Office.)

Refreshments   Cliff Hotel, Ludlow, on the edge of the forest. This has a

continued on page 18

15

Route 2

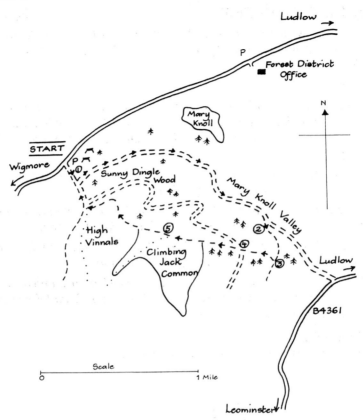

Route 2

Mary Knoll Forest Trail

3½ miles

START *Forestry Commission, Vinnals car park, one mile west of Ludlow on the minor road from Ludlow to Wigmore. OS Sheet 137, GR 474732.*

ROUTE

1. *From the car park take the forestry road and follow the green banded marker posts into the wood. Turn left at the first junction and walk down an undulating road through Sunny Dingle wood into Mary Knoll valley.*

2. *After approximately a mile, just before a tin barn, turn right at the green post and take the track leading uphill.*

3. *At the top of the slope beside the oak coppice turn right into a narrow sunken lane with exposed slabs of rock forming the track.*

4. *Go straight across a forestry road and climb up through conifer woods to the open grassland of Climbing Jack Common.*

5. *Climb up the Common following the green marker posts and bear right on to a narrow track which winds over High Vinnals and down to the Vinnals car park and picnic area.*

ACCESS BY BUS
To Ludlow from Shrewsbury and Hereford.

BUZZARD   shades of brown   54cm

large pleasant garden and welcomes children. Quaint cafés and inns in Ludlow town. (See Route 1.)

THE CURTAIN WALL, CROFT CASTLE

Route 3

Croft Castle and Fishpool Valley

Outline   Croft Castle ~ Old Chestnut Avenue ~ Croft Ambrey Hill Fort ~ Fishpool Valley ~ Croft Castle.

Summary   This is a good family walk on National Trust property following estate paths and grassy tracks. It starts in Croft Castle car park — an attractive paddock outside the castle walls which is an ideal picnic spot for children. The route climbs gently to the Iron Age hill fort with panoramic views over Wales and the Worcestershire plains and then it descends through the steep sided Fishpool Valley beside the little chain of artificial lakes.

Unless you visit the castle the only payment is a small voluntary contribution to the car park.

Attractions   Croft Castle is a Welsh border castle dating from the 15th century. The Croft family were Normans who settled in Herefordshire before the Conquest in the time of Edward the Confessor. There are many stories about the fortunes of the Castle and the family. Lord Croft helped Edward Prince of Wales to escape from Hereford in 1265. Mounted on a white horse he escorted him first to Croft and then to Wigmore Castle. In the Civil War, Sir William Croft fought for the Royalists and after a local skirmish he was pursued as far as his own park where he died. The National Trust own the castle now but members of the Croft family still live on the estate.

The Castle is approached by a beautiful avenue of oaks and beeches and ends before a Gothic curtain-wall — a mini castle which will enchant children.

Croft Ambrey is a Celtic hill fort occupied from the 4th century B.C. to A.D. 50. The inhabitants were cornfarmers and their granaries and storage pits have been discovered on the 8 acre site. When the Romans invaded Britain outer defences were constructed at the fort. The camp probably received refugees rallying to the standards of Caractacus but he was defeated in the Welsh hills in A.D. 50. A Roman garrison was established nearby and Croft Ambrey was abandoned. The views from the hill fort are superb — 14 counties including much of Wales can be seen on a clear day. Can the children imagine they are camp guards in this troubled time when the Romans were marching?

Fishpool Valley was where the inhabitants of the Castle kept their stock of fish for Friday's dinner. Now the pools are quiet and mysterious

continued on page 22

19

Route 3

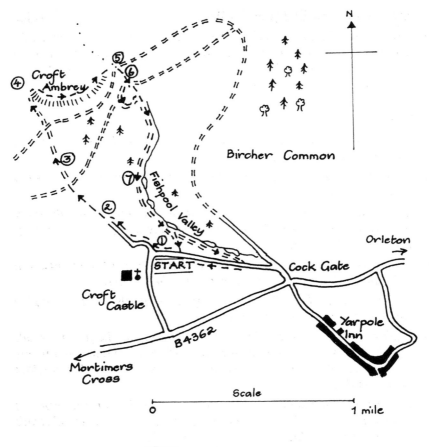

N

Croft Ambrey

④

⑤

⑥

Bircher Common

▲③

⑦

②

Fishpool Valley

①

START

Cock Gate

Orleton

Croft Castle

Yarpole Inn

B4362

Mortimers Cross

Scale

0   1 mile

BARN OWL   light brown and white   34cm

Route 3

Croft Castle and Fishpool Valley $3\frac{1}{2}$ miles

START *Croft Castle car park. At Cock Gate, a small crossroads on the B4362 between Mortimer's Cross and Orleton, follow the National Trust signpost and drive over the cattle grid and up Oak Avenue towards Croft Castle. GR 450654.*

ROUTE

1. *Turn right at the Castle gateway and follow the metalled track, passing an estate house on the left.*

2. *Go through a gate and follow an avenue of old chestnut trees to the top of the meadow.*

3. *Go through another gate marked Croft Ambrey and follow the track through the conifer wood. Continue up to the next gate and bear left round the edge of the fort.*

4. *Go through the entrance to the fort, a cleft in the earth ramparts, and walk along the eastern edge planted with old beeches.*

5. *Follow the track down from the end of the ramparts and go through a small gate in the perimeter fence.*

6. *Walk down the slope into Fishpool Valley crossing the forestry road. (If the path is overgrown beyond the road, turn right and follow the forestry road for a short distance, then loop round to the left to rejoin the original footpath.)*

7. *Keep to the path that runs beside the pools on the right of the stream. (If you wish to shorten the walk at the pumphouse a track on the right leads you back past rhododendrons to the car park.)*

   At the end of the valley turn right up the track to the Castle drive and walk back to your car along the magnificent oak avenue.

reflecting the colours of the surrounding trees. The steep-sided valley was landscaped in the 'Picturesque' style in the late 18th century and the Grotto and the 'Gothick' pumphouse can still still be seen. Perhaps the family can discover the icehouse in the woods where great blocks of ice were stored for food preservation in the days before refrigerators.

There is a variety of wildlife on the estate. Fallow deer inhabit the woods, the rare pied flycatcher nests near the fish pools and the old hornbeams on Croft Ambrey attract hawfinches which eat hornbeam seed with great relish. There are waterbirds such as moorhens and tufted duck at the pools. At dusk tawny owls can be heard in the woods and the family might see a barn owl hunting. (If the family are interested in learning more about the Castle and its wildlife the National Trust have a number of inexpensive publications available at Croft Castle.)

Refreshments The Bell Inn, Yarpole. Garden and picnic tables, climbing frame. Children welcome.

Yarpole Stores, teas in the garden.

Post Office, Yarpole, ice creams.

Barrington Hall N.T., lunches and teas in the old kitchen.

THE MONUMENT

22

Route 4   4 miles
Offa's Dyke and the Monument

Outline   The Monument ~ Offa's Dyke Path ~ Old Impton Farm ~
Taylor's Wood ~ The Monument.

Summary   This walk includes both a fine stretch of Offa's Dyke and a
monument to a local benefactor coming 1,000 years after the Dyke.
From the Dyke there are some of the most breathtaking views in the
whole of the Welsh Borders. The route includes hill walking and a
section through forestry land and a chance to picnic on Offa's Dyke itself.

Attractions   The efforts of two men are honoured on this walk. The
Monument was erected in honour of Sir Richard Green-Price 1803–1887
who was a 'great benefactor to the County of Radnor'. He was a
supporter of the proposals to build the railways to Presteigne, New
Radnor, Knighton and Llandrindod Wells. The inscription says
confidently that his efforts will long outlive his name but sadly the
Presteigne and New Radnor railways were closed in 1958.

   'The formidable King Offa ordered the great rampart to be built
between the Welsh and Mercia from sea to sea' wrote Bishop Asser in his
9th century life of King Alfred. Both constructions involved hard labour!
The navvies toiled to build the railways and stretches of the Dyke were
assigned to individual gangs. For the ditches and ramparts it has been
estimated 4 million man hours would have been required.

   In contrast to the fate of the railways Offa's Dyke has survived
almost intact and has been rejuvenated into a long distance footpath.

   This is border country at its best as you stride down the Dyke. The
wonderful freshness of the air, buzzards wheeling overhead and the soft
rolling hills are an unforgettable experience. The panorama includes the
Malvern Hills, the Black Mountains, the Brecons and the hills of the
Forest of Dean. Can the children see the little sugar loaf hill called the
Whimble? On the first line of hills to your right is the tiny church of
Pilleth with a clump of trees on the hillside above. This is the site of the
battle of Pilleth 1401, in which Owain Glyndŵr who was defending his
principality from the inroads of the English met a force of Herefordshire
men led by Sir Edmund Mortimer and soundly defeated them. The
clump of trees marks the burial place of those killed.

   In Taylors Wood you can often see woodcutters at work preparing
short logs to be used as pit props. The woodland is an ideal habitat for
tawny owls. Look out for goldcrests and yellowhammers.

continued on page 25

23

Route 4

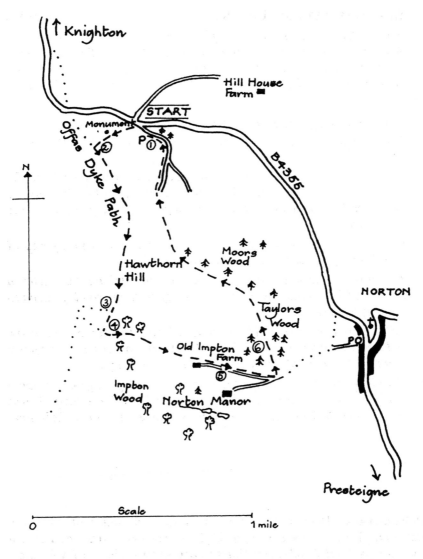

Route 4

Offa's Dyke and the Monument 4 miles

START *Park in a small lane off the B4355 between Norton and Knighton. After passing through the village of Norton the road starts a long climb uphill. Shortly before reaching the top of the hill there is a small lane on the left opposite Hill House farm drive. GR 287687.*

ROUTE

1. *Walk back along the lane for a short distance and enter the field on your left through a gate. Walk up towards the marble monument in the middle of the field.*

2. *Continue towards the gate in the woodland and cross the stile on the left. You are now on Offa's Dyke Path. Turn left and walk along the Dyke until you reach an Offa's Dyke signpost at the point where the Dyke peters out.*

3. *Continue in the same direction for a short distance across the field and then bear left towards a gate in the woodland.*

4. *Pass through the gate and follow the track downhill until it reaches a house and farm buildings. Pass to the left of the house coming out on to a metalled road.*

5. *Follow this lane which overlooks Norton Manor to where a drive on the right makes a hairpin turn to descend to the Manor. Just past this point you take the track off through the wood on your left.*

6. *Follow the track up through the wood and through a gate. Continue along the track with the hedge on your right and eventually it will become metalled and lead you into the little lane where the walk began.*

Refreshments There is no village inn halfway on this walk so take a delicious picnic and have it on the Dyke — you can savour the views at the same time! Hill walking is thirsty work so have plenty of fruit juice. After the walk why not drive to Presteigne for tea and refreshment? There are little cafés and the most wonderful bakery and cake shop — try some pudding cake if you want something sustaining! The Radnorshire Arms used to belong to one of the courtiers of Elizabeth I — it serves delicious cream teas in the garden.

OFFA'S DYKE HERITAGE PARK

FOXGLOVE   purple   June–Sept.

26

Offa's Dyke and Panpunton Hill

Outline Offa's Dyke Centre ~ Skyborry Green ~ Panpunton Hill ~ Offa's Dyke Centre.

Summary The walk starts from the picnic area in the Offa's Dyke Heritage Park and follows the banks of the River Teme. It continues along a lane to the tiny hamlet of Skyborry Green and then climbs to join Offa's Dyke.

There are several alternatives on this walk. Little children will be content with the small excursion along the river especially if it involves a picnic and a paddle or ball game. There is also an adventure playground between the Heritage Centre and the river which can be an incentive for returning walkers.

Perhaps the family would like to scramble up Panpunton Hill to the Dyke and walk a short distance along the Dyke returning by the same route. This is steep! but the views are wonderful and it gives a great sense of achievement. Make sure you have some fruit juice in the rucksacks.

The circular walk also follows the river but it does involve walking along a lane to the hamlet and a steep climb to the Dyke. Then the route follows a level stretch with magnificent views over the surrounding countryside and a descent down Panpunton Hill to the lane and railway bridge.

Attractions Shropshire is border country — for hundreds of years it was disputed land and the scene of fierce raids. The first attempt to settle the frontier between the English and the Welsh was made by Offa King of Mercia A.D. 757–796 when he built the great earthwork to mark the boundary of his kingdom. The construction of the ditch and bank involved the movement of millions of tons of earth and must have taken many years to build. It runs from 'sea to sea' from the estuary of the Dee in the north to the Severn estuary in the south. Now the Dyke has a more peaceful function — that of long distance footpath giving pleasure to English and Welsh ramblers! It runs for 168 miles through some of the most beautiful scenery in the country.

Children love climbing on tumps and walls so hill fort ramparts and Offa's Dyke bank are irresistible. It's fun being king of the castle looking down on the small fields and villages.

The largest town along Offa's Dyke Path is Knighton whose Welsh name Tref-y-Clawdd means the Town by the Dyke. This is the home of

continued on page 30

Route 5

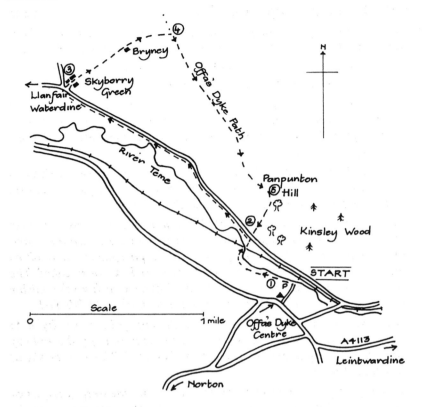

HAREBELL   blue   July–Oct.

Route 5

Offa's Dyke and Panpunton Hill   5 miles

START   *Offa's Dyke Heritage Centre car park, Knighton. Turn off West Street into Crabtree Walk at the side of the Youth Hostel. GR 285726.*

ROUTE   *Not suitable for small children and inexperienced walkers but if you want a challenge and wonderful views climb up to the Dyke.*

1. *Follow the riverside path through the wooded area and into the meadows passing through 3 kissing gates. Cross the river on a wooden footbridge and then cross the railway line with great care. Follow the acorn signs to the lane.*

2. *Turn left here. You pass the entrance drive of Weir Cottage which was where Lord Hunt lived when he was chosen for the first successful Everest expedition. Follow the lane to the junction.*

3. *Turn right in the direction of Clun and Selley Cross. Almost immediately turn right again to follow a track between a farmhouse and outbuildings. Pass Herb Cottage then go through a gateway and follow the track as it climbs the hill. When you reach a house called The Brynny go through a gate at the side and follow a track up the hillside by the hawthorn trees. There is now a steep climb to Offa's Dyke.*

4. *When you reach the footpath turn right and follow the Dyke to Panpunton Hill above Knighton. Can the children spy the railway viaduct on the right and the high mound beside it? This was the site of Knucklas Castle.*

5. *Turn right before you reach the trees and go down the steep grassy track to the lane. Go over the lane and cross the stile and return on the riverside path.*

ACCESS BY BUS
   To Knighton from Ludlow.

the Offa's Dyke Association in the old primary school where there is a very interesting exhibition and a good selection of literature and souvenirs for sale. The walk begins in the riverside park in Knighton which is an ideal area for children. There are picnic tables beside the river and then the path winds between the trees to an open meadow. This is just the spot for a paddle on a hot day! — the mountain water is very clear and cold. Watch out for dippers in the stream. The emblem of the Offa's Dyke path is an acorn and the waymarked path crosses the river on a wooden footbridge and then the railway track itself. This is exciting but take great care. Yellow gorse and delicate blue harebells grow on the Dyke.

Refreshments   Pubs and teashops in Knighton.

THE GATEHOUSE, STOKESAY CASTLE

Route 6

Stokesay Castle and View Edge

Outline   Stokesay Castle ~ Church Way ~ Springhead Gutter ~ View Edge ~ Clapping Wicket ~ Stokesay Castle.

Summary   This walks starts from Stokesay Castle which is open to the public.

It is an interesting building for children to explore and they can spy out the land from the top of the north tower. The route goes over the level crossing and through Stoke Wood, dips into Springhead Gutter and then climbs up to View Edge with a wonderful panorama of hills. The return journey is through the conifer plantation and down the meadows to the level crossing and Stokesay Castle.

Attractions   Stokesay Castle is one of the finest examples of a fortified manor house in England. Licence to crenellate (fortify) was granted in 1291 to Lawrence of Ludlow, a rich wool merchant. During the Civil War it was a Royalist outpost supporting Ludlow but it surrendered with haste to a Parliamentarian force and so escaped undamaged. Today it is under the protection of English Heritage who are carefully restoring the ancient buildings.

There is a legend about two giant brothers who lived overlooking Stokesay Castle, one on Norton Camp, the other on View Edge. They kept their money in a chest under the castle and they used to throw the key to each other from their hill top homes. One day the key fell into the pool. A raven is said to guard the key and the chest but they have not been found!

The Hall at Stokesay is 52 feet long with a fine roof of medieval carpentry supported by three pairs of impressive 'crucks'. Lawrence of Ludlow was rich enough to afford glass in the upper windows but the lower ones were shuttered. Can the children imagine life in medieval times in the Hall at Stokesay? The Hall was the centre of any great house or castle. It was where the lord and his family and servants ate their meals, the lord held his court in the Hall and it was a sleeping place for the servants.

The track between Stokesay and Aldon through Stoke Wood is called Church Way. This was the route used by the Baugh family who lived at Aldon, on their weekly walk to church.

There is a variety of wildlife to be seen on this walk. Rabbits inhabit the fields and banks adjoining the railway and the family might glimpse a

continued on page 34

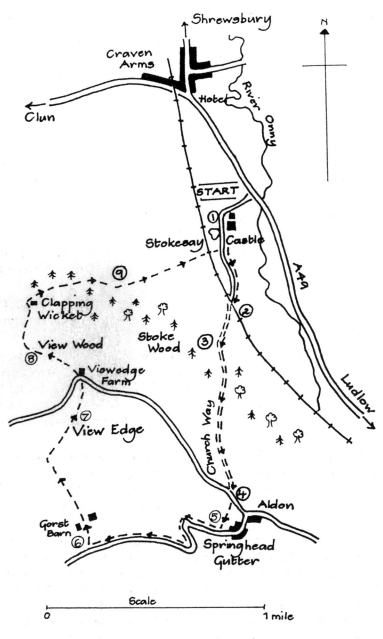

Scale

0   1 mile

Route 6

Stokesay Castle and View Edge

4½ miles

START   *Stokesay Castle car park. A small lane leads to Stokesay Castle from the A49 Shrewsbury to Ludlow road on the outskirts of Craven Arms. GR 435817. (This walk has been waymarked by the County Council as route 1a.)*

ROUTE

1. *Follow the lane from the Castle passing a large pool on the right and continue to the railway crossing.*

2. *Go through the wicket gate and cross the line with great care. Follow the track left to a gate and stile. Go over the stile and turn right up the hedgerow to the next gate and stile.*

3. *Go over the stile and follow the path uphill into Stoke Wood. Follow this track (Church Way) to the road.*

4. *On reaching the road turn left and go over the stile by the signpost on the right before Aldon. Follow the hedge on the left to a stile by a gate and out on to the lane.*

5. *Follow the lane down into Springhead Gutter. Continue uphill for another half mile to a footpath sign at a track on the right leading to Gorst Barn.*

6. *Follow the track to Gorst Barn. Go through the yard and continue through gates into a field. Follow the hedge on the right then go downhill and across the corner of the field to double gates. Continue through these and walk straight uphill across the field to go over a stile in the boundary. Turn right along this to a stile into the next field. You are now on View Edge.*

7. *Cross the corner of the field to a stile by woodland and continue to the next stile and out on to the lane. Turn left then immediately right between the fence and View Edge Farm and along to the stile into View Wood. Follow the path through the woodland and emerge into an open field.*

8. *Keep the wood on the right and follow it round before re-entering through a gateway by a waymark post. Follow the track through woodland before again emerging into an open field. Keep the wood on the right and follow it round and then down to a corner by Clapping Wicket House. Cross the stile into the conifer plantation and follow the path through Stoke Wood. Indian file here on the narrow path!*

9. *At the waymark post turn left out of the wood and go over a stile into a*

field. Bear right across the fields and over stiles to Stokesay Crossing Cottage. Cross the railway line with great care and go along the track to a gate by the lane. Turn left along the lane to the car park.

ACCESS BY BUS
To Craven Arms from Ludlow and Church Stretton.

---

fox in this area. Springhead Gutter is the home of the ravens. Buzzards fly over the hills on View Edge and there are moorhens and coots on Stokesay Pool and sometimes a solitary heron.

There is a real panorama of hills from View Edge which well deserves its name. To the west is the Clun valley and Bury Ditches, the Long Mynd in the north and the Clee Hills and the Malverns in the east.

The little church adjoining the castle is worth a visit. In 1646 a Royalist party took refuge with their horses in the Church but they were driven out by the Parliamentarians who had taken possession of the castle. Can the children find the mounting block by the lychgate? This goes back to the times when parishioners rode on horseback to church.

Refreshments Teas at the Castle Gateway served in the Courtyard.
Stokesay Castle Hotel, Craven Arms, large garden and play area.

A ROUND HOUSE, ASTON ON CLUN

The Arbor Tree

Outline   Hopesay Common ~ Arbor Tree, Aston on Clun ~ Kangaroo Inn, Burrow Wood ~ Round Oak ~ Wart Hill ~ Hopesay Common.

Summary   This is an energetic walk over beautiful wooded and undulating hills and the short climb to the trig point on Wart Hill is rewarded with a magnificent panorama. There is peace and tranquillity these quiet Shropshire villages and hamlets and the Arbor Tree in Aston on Clun with flags fluttering in the breeze is a fascinating sight for children.

Attractions   At the centre of Aston on Clun near the bridge stands a large black poplar tree decked with flags. It is decorated on May 29th each year — Oak Apple Day when many trees are decorated in honour of Charles II's escape from the Roundheads after the Battle of Worcester. The Aston celebrations have nothing to do with the fugitive king but to honour a local girl who married the Squire in 1786. The villagers decorated the tree for the wedding and the Squire is said to have given each family one sovereign on every subsequent anniversary to decorate the tree. The custom has been carried on ever since and the flags flutter bravely all through the year.

On Arbor Day the flags attached to larch poles are nailed to the trunk of the poplar tree and a pageant leads a mock bride and groom to the tree where there is dancing and jollity. The tree is dressed with the Union Jack, the flags of England, Ireland, Scotland and Wales and those of the armed forces and the Commonwealth countries. Can the children identify the different flags?

The village also possesses two Round Houses. Their origin is unknown, unless like similar ones in Cornwall it is to keep the Devil from the corners. The Gothic village inn is called the Kangaroo, reputedly the only inn in England with this name. It is believed the name was changed to Kangaroo by a former landlord who had visited Australia. The Forge Garage was once the blacksmith's shop and it is still owned and operated by the old blacksmith.

Look out for buzzards in Cabin Woods, circling and gliding above the trees. Their wing span is an incredible 120 cm. Listen for their distinctive mewing cries.

Water Hill is one of the finest viewpoints in the area with views over the Long Mynd and the Stiperstones, Wenlock Edge and the Clee Hills.

continued on page 38

35

Route 7

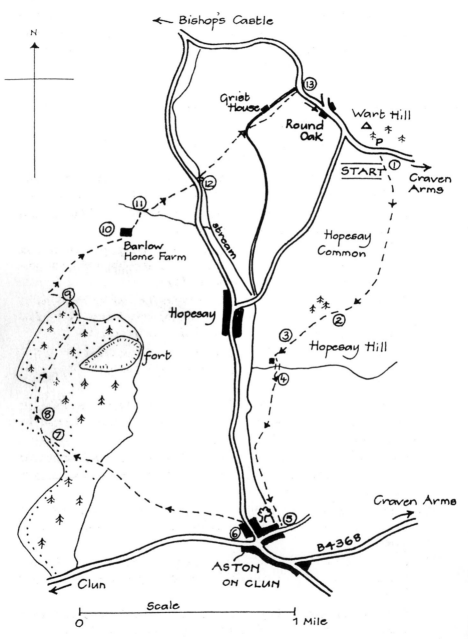

N

← Bishop's Castle

Grieb House

Round Oak

Wart Hill

START ①

Craven Arms

⑬

⑫

⑪

⑩

Barlow Home Farm

stream

Hopesay Common

Hopesay

fort

Hopesay Hill

③

④

②

⑨

⑧

⑦

Craven Arms

⑤

⑥

ASTON ON CLUN

B4368

← Clun

Scale

0   1 Mile

36

Route 7

The Arbor Tree   7 miles

START *At the Forestry car park at Wart Hill, opposite Hopesay Common on Long Lane, a minor road between Craven Arms and Bishops Castle. GR 402845.*

ROUTE

1. Cross the road and go through the gate opposite. Follow the track leading up to Hopesay Common.

2. Keep to the middle of the Common passing a clump of fir trees on your right and walk to a line of old hawthorns.

3. Go down to a corner of the Common and pass through a gate. The track continues down beside a cottage and crosses a footbridge.

4. Climb up the right-hand side of the sloping field and follow an old track through the fields to Aston on Clun.

5. Turn right on the road and walk through the village past the Round House to the bridge and the Arbor Tree. (For the village shop and the Kangaroo Inn turn left at the crossroads.)

6. To continue the walk, turn right at the bridge taking the road to Hopesay. Turn left on to a footpath beside a white bungalow. Follow this track through the fields and up to the conifer woods.

7. Climb through the woods to crosstracks, turn right and take the first track going downhill. At the bottom turn right along the edge of the wood.

8. Fork right, climbing again and take the next left fork downhill this time. There is now a short steep climb bearing right up through the wood near the fence.

9. Climb the stile at the top and, bearing left, head diagonally across the field to a gate and on to a wide track. Turn right and follow the track down to Barlow Home Farm.

10. Follow the main track through the farmyard over the last cattle grid and then turn left and cross into a field sloping steeply down to a small stream.

11. Cross the stream and join a clear track going to the right. Go through a gate and then walk diagonally right across the fields down to a gate by a lane.

12. Cross the lane to a track opposite and walk beside the stream and over a footbridge by a cottage. Continue straight ahead and climb the open

land between the trees to the top of the hill. Go through the gate at the top and walk down the right-hand hedge to the track. Turn left and go through the gate on the right into the field beside the track to Grist House. Walk parallel with this track to reach the lane.

13. *Turn right, passing through the tiny hamlet of Round Oak and follow the road back to the Forestry car park.*

    If the family would like to see the panorama of hills make the short climb to Wart Hill.

On a clear day you can see the outlines of the Malverns in the east and Cader Idris in the west. Hopesay Common owned by the National Trust is an ideal place for a picnic — sheep and gentle shaggy ponies graze on the short turf.

Refreshments The Kangaroo Inn, Aston on Clun. Children welcome, play area. Extra supplies may be purchased from the well-stocked village shop.

BURY DITCHES

Route 8   1¼ miles

Bury Ditches

Outline   Car park and picnic area ~ Bury Ditches fort ~ Viewpoint ~ picnic area.

Summary   This is a perfect walk for a family with very young children. The steep climb from Clunton is done by car and the walk starts from a wooded car park and picnic area. It is only a short distance to the hill fort which has magnificent views. Young walkers will feel they are on top of the world! The trail leaves the hill fort and curves gently round the hill through woodland of oaks, silver birches and beeches. (There are two other forest trails starting from the car park — Sunnyhill Walk 1¾ miles and Withins Walk 3¼ miles.)

Attractions   Clunton, Clunbury,
　　　　　　　Clungunford and Clun
　　　　　　　Are the quietest places
　　　　　　　under the sun.
　　　　This description by Housman in his poem A Shropshire Lad is still very true today. The Clun villages along the winding river are peaceful country places but these green hills and valleys have not always been so peaceful. The numerous hill forts and Norman Castles are evidence of a more violent age.

Shropshire is famous for its Iron Age hill forts dating from about 600 B.C. The forts were permanently occupied — perhaps a better description would be 'hill top towns'. They had deep ditches and high ramparts topped with a stockade and inside there were many round and rectangular huts. Bury Ditches was a major settlement of farmsteads. Today it is still possible to see the defences — two ramparts on the south and four on the north. These were built in several stages over the life of the settlement. The occupants now are the sturdy black-faced sheep who graze the windswept ramparts.

Bury Ditches is owned by the Forestry Commission who have laid out three trails around the hill fort and the children will enjoy spotting the colour-coded posts. Blue markers point the way round the Bury Ditches walk. There are picnic tables in the little car park among the trees and a bench at the viewpoint half way round. In summer the track to the fort goes through a mass of foxgloves standing like sentries on guard. This is buzzard country — the children can climb the ramparts and scan the horizon to spot their graceful flight.

continued on page 41

39

Route 8

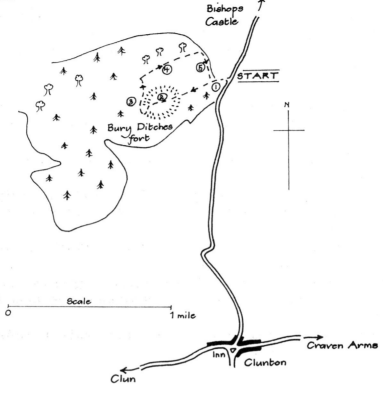

Bishops Castle

START

N

④ ⑤

③ ②

①

Bury Ditches fort

Scale

0   1 mile

Inn

Clun

Clunton

Craven Arms

Welsh Cakes

6 oz margarine
2 oz lard
4 oz currants
1 lb self raising flour
pinch salt
$\frac{1}{4}$ tsp mixed spice
$\frac{1}{4}$ tsp ground nutmeg
7 oz caster sugar
2 eggs
a little milk to mix

Blend the margarine and lard together. Wash and dry the currants. Sieve the flour, salt and spices into a mixing bowl, then rub in the fats. Stir in the sugar and currants. Lightly beat the eggs and mix into the dry ingredients adding enough milk to mix to a firm dough.

Knead lightly on a floured surface, then roll out to a thickness of 1 cm ($\frac{1}{2}$ inch). Cut into rounds using a floured 5 cm (2 inch) fluted cutter. Cook on both sides to a golden brown, on a moderately hot pre-heated griddle or in a strong, heavy based frying pan.

Route 8

Bury Ditches   1¼ miles

START   *In Clunton take the minor road to Brockton opposite the Inn. In about 1¾ miles the road reaches the wood and the picnic area. GR 327837.*

ROUTE

1. *This walk follows the blue marker posts and is called the Bury Ditches walk. From the picnic area take the higher track up the slope to the hill fort.*

2. *The track goes through the original entrance to the hill fort and over the summit.*

3. *Descend to a gate and stile on the far side. Cross the stile and turn right along the track. Follow this path to the viewpoint seat at the junction and turn right.*

4. *Follow the path downwards and where it curves left take the track through oaks, silver birches and beeches.*

5. *Pass a gate with the Shropshire Way buzzard, turn right up the slope through the pine trees and rejoin the original track to return to the picnic area.*

Perhaps the family would like to return to Bury Ditches to explore one of the other trails.

As this is a short expedition why not combine it with a trip to Clun to have delicious Welsh cakes in the Clun Bridge Tearooms and to explore the Norman Castle. This was a real fortress, the site of many battles with Welsh raiding parties. The remaining tower which formed the living quarters was 80 feet high with walls 11 feet thick!

Refreshments   The Crown Inn, Clunton.
       Hundred House, Purslow.

41

WILD PONIES ON KERRY RIDGEWAY

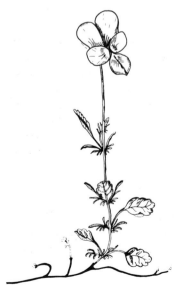

MOUNTAIN PANSY   violet/yellow   May–Aug.

42

The Kerry Ridgeway and the Cantlin Stone

Outline   Crossways ~ Shadwell Hill ~ Cantlin Stone ~ Kerry Ridgeway
~ Barretts Farm ~ Crossways.

Summary   This is one of the wilder Shropshire walks with an exciting
feeling of remoteness and shadowy figures from the past. It begins on
high moorland and climbs up past the Pedlar's Grave to the ancient
Kerry Ridgeway Drovers' Road. This is the boundary between England
and Wales and the views are wonderful on a clear day. The walk
continues through forestry plantations and over moorland where curlews
call and then descends to the patchwork of little fields, streams and
farms.

Attractions   Children will be intrigued to step along a track that traders
and animals have used for 4,000 years with Wales on one side and
England on the other. Can they spy the Cantlin stone as they climb
Shadwell Hill? This is a flat limestone slab bearing the inscription WC
Dcsd here 1691 Buried at Betvs. The initials stand for William Cantlin a
travelling pedlar who collapsed and died at this spot in 1691. There was
an argument among the neighbouring parishes as to who was responsible
for burying the stranger but finally Bettws-s-Crwyn gave him a grave in
their churchyard. Sadly the stone lies neglected now and a carved cross
set up by Beriah Botfield, a member of Parliament for Ludlow, has fallen
beside the stone.

    The Kerry Ridgeway is an ancient track dating back to the early
Bronze Age about 2,000 BC — often described as the oldest road in
Wales. It was a trading route with traders carrying rough axeheads
eastwards from the Axe factory on Corndon Hill and flint tools
westwards. In the Middle Ages the Kerry Ridgeway became one of the
great Welsh drove roads for the cattle farmers of north Wales. It
remained an important drove road until the railways came to this area in
the 1850's. The Ridgeway is now the national boundary between
England and Wales.

    Where the track bears right and leaves the Kerry Ridgeway there is a
wonderful place for a picnic on the edge of the moorland.

    After exploring such a remote part of Shropshire children will enjoy
returning to Clun for light refreshment. There is a free car park beside
the river opposite the little Post Office. Families can have their own
picnic on a seat by the river or be tempted by the homemade delights of

continued on page 46

43

Route 9

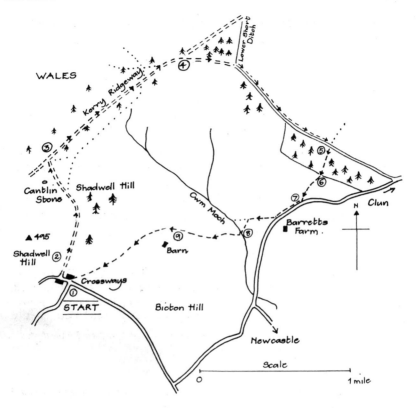

WALES

Korry Ridgeway

Lower Short Ditch

④

③

Canblin Stone

Shadwell Hill

▲ 495

Cwm Moch

⑤

⑥

N Clun

⑦

Barretts Farm

Shadwell Hill ②

⑧

⑨

Barn

Crossways ①

START

Bicton Hill

Newcastle

Scale

O   1 mile

Route 9

The Kerry Ridgeway and the Cantlin Stone   6 miles

START   *Crossways. A hamlet 2½ miles NW of Newcastle on Clun on a minor road. Park near the cattle grid GR 204858.*

ROUTE

1. *Continue westwards along the lane passing Crossways Cottage on your right, to a forestry track on the right. Follow this, passing the Forestry Commission sign 'Ceri' on your left.*

2. *Climb up the track passing young spruce and fir. Pass through 2 gates and when the track turns right keep straight on along the open hill-top. As you near conifers again you will see the Cantlin Stone on your left near the track surrounded by a short wooden fence. (The trig point on Shadwell Hill is off the public footpath SW of the stone. The height is 495 m and the views are wonderful on a clear day.)*

3. *Turn right and follow the track for about ¾ mile.*

4. *The track leaves the plantation edge and bears right entering the woodland. As you turn look for Stapeley Hill, Corndon and the Stiperstones on the left. Keep to this good forestry track until it joins a tarmac lane and continue along the lane leaving the trees again. When there is a valley on your left and a plantation on your right look for a grassy 'ride' through the trees on your right.*

5. *Follow the ride to a gate at the edge of the trees.*

6. *Cross the gate and go down the hillside bearing slightly right to reach the lane by a gate in the corner of the field.*

7. *Turn right along the lane until you reach a farm on your left. Shortly after the second entrance to the farm turn right through a gate on to an old track. The track goes down through another gate. Shortly afterwards turn left through a gate on your left and go down the field to a stream.*

8. *Cross the stream and turn right immediately. Walk uphill to a gate in a hedge between 2 telegraph poles. Go through the gate and bear left up the hill to reach a fence on your left. At the fence turn right and follow the fence, passing through one more gate on your way.*

9. *Through the gate keep the fence on your left but when you reach another gate in this fence pass through it. You will see a large metal barn in the field you have entered. Bear right, away from the barn, contouring the hillside and making for some trees on the horizon.*

45

As you cross the hillside you should see a hedge. Head for this and, on reaching it, keep it to your left and pass through a wicket gate and 2 more gates. Enter the lane by a gate near the cattle grid and the start.

———

the Clun Bridge Tea Rooms. This is a cosy little teashop open from Easter to October each year. Around the walls are watercolour scenes by local artists.

Clun is a very ancient town and the old stone bridge with its low arches was originally a medieval packhorse bridge. There is a local saying that 'whoever crosses Clun Bridge comes home sharper than he went' but whether this means they were chased back sharply by the Welsh or that they returned wiser is not known.

Refreshments Clun Bridge Tea Rooms.
Clun, Sun Inn, patio.

MITCHELL'S FOLD

Route 10
Mitchell's Fold — the Stone Circle

$4\frac{1}{2}$ miles

Outline   Priestweston village ~ Mitchell's Fold ~ Stapeley Hill ~ Marton Lane ~ Priestweston.

Summary   This walk is on good paths and tracks. The route follows a sunken lane from the village of Priestweston to the high track above Cwm Dingle with wonderful views of Cader Idris and the Aran mountains in the west. The track leads on to the open hillside and the mysterious stone circle and then climbs gently to the cairns on Stapeley Hill with a view of the Stiperstones and the abandoned mines. The return route is a gradual descent on grassy tracks to Marton Lane and then to Priestweston.

Attractions   There is a magical quality about this part of Shropshire especially at the mysterious stone circle on the high moorland. It was built 3,500 years ago by the Bronze Age people and it may have been connected with sun worship because it stands in an exposed place open to the rays of the rising and setting sun. A description of the circle written in 1752 says that two of the stones supported a third stone like the lintels of Stonehenge but this has toppled to the ground long ago. The remains of a Bronze Age axe factory have been found nearby, below Corndon Hill.

  Children will enjoy the legend of Mitchells Fold which tells the story of a famine and how the Fairy Queen sent a beautiful cow to Stapeley Hill to produce milk for everyone. Only one pail a day was allowed but the local witch called Mitchell was determined to break the spell. She went to the hill at dead of night and milked the cow into a pail with a sieve at the bottom. The cow was puzzled because the pail never became full but a storm arose and a flash of lightning showed her the wasted milk on the grass. The cow gave an enormous kick and tossed the witch head over heels. The cow disappeared but Mitchell was turned to stone and when the villagers arrived next day they placed other stones in a circle around her to make sure she would never escape!

  During the summer months look for the beautiful yellow mountain pansies on Stapeley Hill. This hill is 403 metres high. Can the children spot the Cow Stone, a great dark stone half buried in the ground? This is where the cow of the legend was buried. Enjoy the panoramic view of the Welsh mountains, the Stiperstones ridge and Corndon Hill and Lan Fawr. Lapwings and curlews glide over the moorland making plaintive cries. Listen to the 'peewit' flight call of the lapwing and the 'quee quee quee cooorwee' song of the curlew.

continued on page 50

47

Route 10

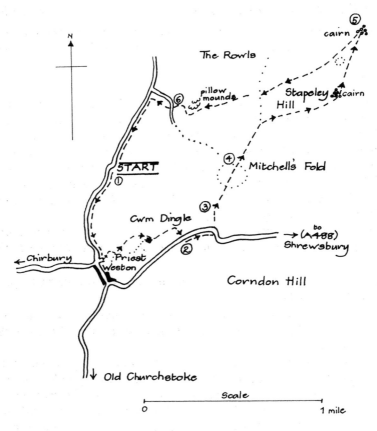

N

The Rowls

cairn ⑤

pillow
mounds

⑥

Stapeley ⚡cairn
Hill

④↗ Mitchell's Fold

START
①

Cwm Dingle

③↗

to
→(A488)
Shrewsbury

②

←Chirbury

Priest
Weston

Corndon Hill

↓ Old Churchstoke

Scale

0   1 mile

48

Route 10

Mitchell's Fold — Stone Circle 4½ miles

START   *Marton Lane — a minor road between Priestweston and Marton. There are several parking places near Priestweston village. GR 292962.*

ROUTE

1. *Walk along Marton Lane into Priestweston and opposite the turning to Chirbury take the track on your left. This sunken lane passes an old Methodist chapel, now a private home, and climbs steadily out of the village. Join another track at a T junction and turn left. (The bank along this quiet path is an ideal place for a picnic with wonderful views of the Welsh mountains.) Join a wider track by a cottage and a new bungalow and turn left. Below you lies Cwm Dingle — cwm is the Welsh name for valley.*

2. *The track joins a tarmac lane. Turn left and after about 50 yards turn left again on to a track. An English Heritage sign points the way to the Stone Circle.*

3. *Continue over a stile and on to the open hillside. Follow the grassy path through the bracken to the Stone Circle.*

4. *From the Stone Circle you can see on your right the first cairn on Stapeley Hill. Head towards this and then walk the short distance to the northern cairn.*

5. *Turn back towards the southern cairn but veer to the right and descend the slope. Cross the wide grassy track and head slightly uphill making for a fence on top of the next hill which is The Rowls. (On your right is an ancient warren, artificial burrows where rabbits were kept and bred — described as Pillow Mounds on the O.S. map.) At the fence bear left keeping the fence on your right and follow the path which widens into a track. A valley opens below you on your left. Where the track veers left take the fainter track to the right with a rocky outcrop slightly above you on your right. Descend gradually and join another track by an old stone wall. Go through a gate and continue on the track to a tarmac lane.*

6. *Cross the lane and take the left hand of 2 gates into a field. Cross the field keeping the hedge on your right. Go through another gate and field with the hedge still on your right and enter the lane through a gate in the hedge. Turn left and follow the lane back to Priestweston.*

ACCESS BY BUS

To Priestweston from Churchstoke and Shrewsbury.

Refreshments The Oak Tree Inn, Old Churchstoke. 1 mile south. Open all day for refreshments and little adventure garden. Children welcome. The Old Miner's Arms, Priestweston.

THE STIPERSTONES

COTTON GRASS

The Stiperstones and the Devil's Chair

Outline   The Bog ~ Cranberry Rock ~ Devil's Chair ~ Shepherd's Rock ~ Perkins Beach ~ Stiperstones Village ~ The Bog.

Summary   The area around the Stiperstones is old mining country once extensively mined for lead and barytes. The walk starts from the site of the Bog Mine and climbs Stiperstones Hill to the rocky tors above. There are panoramic views from the Stiperstones and the ridge walk passes a rock known as the Devil's Chair. Stout shoes and a stout heart are needed for this expedition into witches territory! The descent is down a winding valley or batch known as Perkins Beach, the site of a smaller mine. This leads into Stiperstones village and to the Stiperstones Inn. There is a short climb on to the lower slopes of the hill and then the route follows a straight track west of the Stiperstones gently descending to the car park.

    Not recommended for children under 9. For families with very young children for whom the walk might be too arduous an interesting alternative would be a picnic near Cranberry Rock parking area and a walk up the grassy track to explore the Stiperstones.

Attractions   The Bog mine was worked from the mid 18th century until the 1880's and it was once a thriving community of 200 people. The little school is now a field study centre and on the site of the old miners' institute adjoining the Bog car park there is a very interesting display of information and rock samples.

    The Stiperstones are very ancient rocks. 500 million years ago the ridge was a beach of pure quartz sand and pebbles. Volcanic eruptions folded the Stiperstones Quartz at a steep angle and the freezing action of the last Ice Age reduced it to a jagged line of tors.

    The Stiperstones is Mary Webb country, a wild mysterious landscape steeped in legend. This is the legendary meeting place of the Shropshire witches! The highest of the rocks is called the Devil's Chair. One story says the Devil was making his way from Ireland, his apron full of stones to fill up Hells Gutter (Shropshire for ravine) on the other side of the hill. He sat down on the Devil's Chair for a rest. When he got up his apron strings broke and all the stones scattered around where they remain to this day!

    From the summit the views are breathtaking and on a clear day it is possible to see Cader Idris in the Welsh mountains. There is a

continued on page 54

Route 11

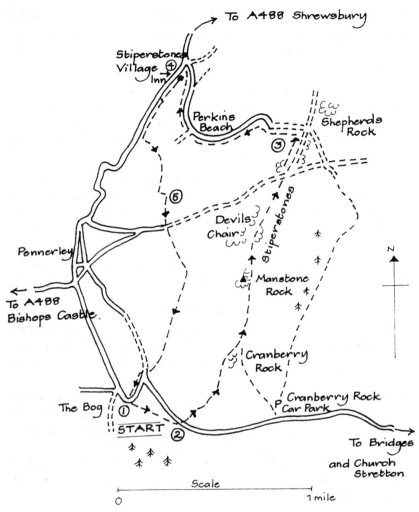

To A488 Shrewsbury

Stiperstones Village Inn ④

Perkins Beach

Shepherds Rock

③

⑤

Devils Chair

Stiperstones

Pennerley

To A488 Bishops Castle.

Manstone Rock

Cranberry Rock

Cranberry Rock Car Park

The Bog ①

START ②

To Bridges and Church Stretton.

N

Scale

0   1 mile

Route 11

The Stiperstones and the Devil's Chair   6 miles

START   *The lower of the two car park and picnic areas on the site of the Bog Mine. GR 356979.*

ROUTE

1. *Cross the car park uphill towards the road to the footpath sign. Follow the track alongside a pool and turn left uphill through rough scrub to a stile. Keep straight on to the next stile following an old hedge boundary. Follow the same line to the second stile, then bear slightly left to the stile by the gate and out on to the road.*

2. *Go through the gate and on to the track opposite, then over the stile onto Stiperstones Hill by the Nature Conservancy notice board. Climb uphill to the left of Cranberry Rock. Follow the path right, round the rock, to join the main stony track. Continue along the ridge, passing Manstone Rock and the Devil's Chair.*

3. *Keep to the path along the ridge past Scattered Rock towards Shepherd's Rock (last large rocky outcrop). Just before reaching Shepherd's Rock turn left and follow a track downhill. Proceed down the valley, passing the old mine workings and ruined cottages at Perkins Beach. Keep downhill, ignoring the fork to the left, passing two white cottages. This track eventually leads into Stiperstones village. Turn left on to the minor road past a small Post Office and the Stiperstones Inn.*

4. *Proceed to the end of the village to a footpath sign on the left which leads round the back of a private garage and over a stile. Follow the field boundary on your right uphill. Where the field narrows bear left to the stile and Nature Conservancy board in a parallel fence. Follow the route uphill through gorse, coming out on to the lower slopes of Stiperstones Hill. Continue uphill, ignoring tracks off, until the fields end and open moorland is reached.*

5. *Turn right and follow the track along the field boundary on your right. Follow the track ignoring all turnings until reaching a stile. Cross this stile and two more and go diagonally right downhill to a fourth stile before joining the road on a hairpin bend. Continue downhill to the Bog Mine parking area.*

ACCESS BY BUS

To The Bog from Shrewsbury.

triangulation station on the top of Manstone Rock and it is fun identifying the distinctive shapes of the Wrekin, the Malverns and the Black Mountains.

Watch out for ravens, kestrels and buzzards over the ridge. Small brown meadow pipits dart among the heather. Small wild flowers grow on Stiperstone Hill — heath bedstraw, cow wheat, mountain pansy and betony. An unusual plant growing in the wetter patches is cotton grass with large fluffy seed heads.

There was a small mine at Perkins Beach (the name derives from batch meaning an open space near a river) and the walk passes along the high street of a village now marked only by piles of rubble and old garden hedgerows.

Around the Stiperstones and the Long Mynd in the 1860's school holidays began when the bilberries were ripe and the children did not return to school until there were no more berries to pick. If you visit in late Summer your family can have fun collecting the fruit which makes a delicious pie, but school must start on time!

Refreshments   The Stiperstones Inn welcomes children and serves good food all day from 10 a.m. Families can enjoy a snack in the garden or inside the Inn.

THE HORSESHOE INN, BRIDGES

Route 12
Darnford Valley and Bridges

5½ miles

Outline   Wild Moor ~ Ratlinghope ~ Bridges ~ Darnford Brook ~ Wild Moor.

Summary   The walk starts on the heights of the Long Mynd and descends to the little hamlet of Ratlinghope. It then follows Darnford Brook to Bridges and refreshment at the Horseshoe Inn beside the stream. The return journey through the peaceful river valley is a wonderful opportunity to observe river and moorland birds. The final part of this walk is along a narrow moorland lane but an alternative walk for young children to include only the river walk would be to park at the Inn at Bridge and to do a linear walk along the Darnford brook. A riverside picnic could be enjoyed before retracing your steps.

Attractions   There is a variety of birdlife in this quiet valley and it is a wonderful place to visit in Springtime. In the pine wood there are tiny goldcrests, willow warblers and chiffchaffs. Watch the stream for kingfishers, dippers and herons and listen for the calls of the buzzard and the raven as they fly overhead. Wild Moor is said to be haunted but perhaps you should not relate this information! Take heart, you are never far from the little lane to Ratlinghope. The antics of the rabbit population are very amusing to watch on the moorland and the children might see a stoat chasing a rabbit over the short turf.

From the little church in Ratlinghope the Rev. D. Carr tried to walk back over the Long Mynd in mid winter to his home at Woolstaston. The churches are 12 miles apart by road but only 4 miles 'over the top'. Even in 1865 the practice of sharing rectors was in operation and Mr Carr served Woolstaston and Ratlinghope. On 29th January 1865 the snow was deeper than it had been for many years. The folk at Ratlinghope pleaded with Rev. Carr to stay the night but he set out on the return trip and got lost in a blizzard for 24 hours. He lost his hat, coat, boots and stick but he struggled on and survived. He wrote the story of his adventures in a little booklet 'A night in the snow', the proceeds of which paid for a carved font in Woolstaston Church. The booklet has been reprinted so perhaps the family would like to read the story of this epic journey! (Available from the National Trust shop, Cardingmill Valley.)

Refreshments   The Horseshoe Inn at Bridges is very picturesque and sometimes there are trekking ponies hitched to the trees by the stream. In Summer the family can enjoy cold drinks and refreshment sitting outside.

Route 12

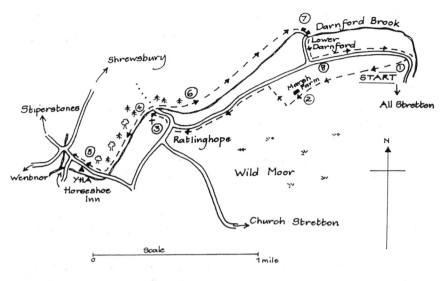

DIPPER   brown/chestnut/white   18cm

56

Route 12

Darnford Valley and Bridges   5½ miles

START   *Wild Moor, near Upper Darnford farm, on the minor road between Ratlinghope and All Stretton. Parking near the National Trust sign. GR 427975.*

ROUTE

1. *Follow the hedgeline uphill across the moor for a short distance. The path and the hedge part company but keep straight ahead and you will join up again.*

2. *Pass the ruin of Marsh Farm on your right and then turn right over a stile. Walk straight down the field to a gate by some large beeches. Turn left along the lane.*

3. *In Ratlinghope turn right by the church and follow the track down to a ford. Cross the stream and turn left into the wood (Shropshire Way sign).*

4. *Follow the track through the pine wood, across a field and through a gate. Continue through the wood by the stream to an iron gate by the lane.*

5. *Turn right and walk along the lane to Bridges and the Horseshoe Inn, passing the Youth Hostel on the way. After refreshment at Bridges retrace your steps to the ford. Instead of crossing the ford go straight across the track and stay on the path with the stream on your right.*

6. *Continue along the grassy track and turn left up the valley, following the Shropshire Way signs.*

7. *When you reach some large barns turn right downhill. Cross over the footbridge, passing barns and a cottage and follow the track to a lane.*

8. *Turn left along the lane and follow it to Upper Darnford.*

ASHES HOLLOW

Ashes Hollow and Pole Bank

Outline   Little Stretton ~ Ashes Valley ~ Pole Bank ~ Round Hill ~ Callow Hill ~ Little Stretton.

Summary   This is one of the most picturesque and exciting walks on the Long Mynd. It begins in the village of Little Stretton and follows the stream through a rocky valley to the top of the plateau. The walk continues to the highest point on the Long Mynd with magnificent panoramic views and then descends gently on a wide grassy track to the little village and civilisation.

Attractions   The Long Mynd is a natural barrier between England and Wales, a great whale-back ridge covered with heather and bracken stretching nearly 10 miles. The windswept moors are a wonderful area for walking with a feeling of wildness and freedom. Mynd is Welsh for mountain and the narrow valleys which cut into its sides are known locally as batches or hollows.

    In stormy winter weather the range can be a dangerous place and the last fair of the year held at Church Stretton used to be called 'Dead Man's Fair' because of the number of men who died trying to reach home over the hills. In January 1865 the Rev. Donald Carr took 24 hours to fight his way home after conducting a service in another valley.

    Watch out for ravens performing acrobatics in the sky uttering their deep croak and soaring buzzards mewing to each other. The ring ouzel — the mountain blackbird — visits the wild upper valleys in Summer — perhaps the children will see him in Ashes Hollow. He has a white bib and a distinctive loud high note repeated several times.

    By the sides of the streams grow bog moss and the delicate pink bog pimpernel. Sundew and butterwort are two insectivorous plants — they trap insects on their leaves and digest them to make up for the poor soil!

    There is a scenic direction stone (toposcope) on Pole Bank the highest point of the Long Mynd. Can the children spot Cader Idris, the Brecon Beacons and the Black Mountains. The Long Mynd is the setting for Malcolm Savilles Lone Pine stories. It would be fun for older children to read the exciting adventure tales Mystery at Witchend and Wings over Witchend before or after their visit. The Lone Pine club was founded at a lonely house called Witchend in a hidden valley of the Long Mynd.

    Descending the grassy track to Little Stretton you will see the great hill of Caer Caradoc. This is thought to be the spot where the British

continued on page 62

Route 13

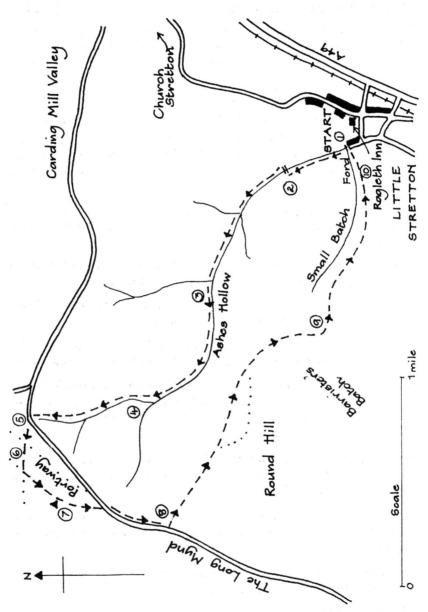

Route 13

Ashes Hollow and Pole Bank   5½ miles

START   *Little Stretton village just west of the A49 south of Church Stretton. Park in the small lane beside the brook. (Take the lane alongside the Ragleth Inn and bear right at the brook.) GR 442918.*

ROUTE

1. *Follow the lane to the ford and cross the stream by the footbridge. Immediately cross the stile on your right and go through 2 fields.*

2. *Pass the National Trust sign. Cross the stream again by another footbridge and turn left into the valley. The stream is now on your left. Take care as the valleysides become steeper and the path becomes narrow.*

3. *At the first meeting of the streams follow the stream flowing from the left. The valley becomes wider and the stream has to be crossed several times.*

4. *Keep to the right at the next meeting of the streams. The path becomes narrower and climbs steadily to the head of the valley.*

5. *Turn left at the wooden waymark post on to a metalled road. Almost immediately turn right on to a stony track.*

6. *Ignore the first paths which cross the track. Turn left at the 4 wooden posts and walk up to Pole Bank the highest point of the Long Mynd.*

7. *Continue on the path in the same direction until you reach 4 more wooden posts and the metalled road. Turn right and continue along the road to a wooden waymark post on your left marked Little Stretton.*

8. *Turn left off the road and follow the broad track down the hill. Where the track forks go left. Pass 3 hawthorn trees on your right and follow the path round the hillside.*

9. *When the track meets a fence and gate turn left and go down into Small Batch keeping the fence on your right. Descend with care if the path is wet.*

10. *Go through a gate at the bottom which may be muddy, pass a cottage on your left and cross the ford again.*

ACCESS BY BUS

    To Little Stretton from Church Stretton and Ludlow.

leader Caradoc (Caractacus) made his final stand against the Romans. In Little Stretton there are timber-framed houses, tiny waterfalls and miniature bridges over the stream. Have the children ever seen a thatched church? Walk into the village to see the picturesque black and white building.

Refreshments The Ragleth Arms, garden. The younger members of the family may enjoy sitting at an old school desk in the garden.

The Green Dragon, garden. Children's menu.

THE CRUCK HOUSE, MINTON

Minton Green and Callow Hollow

Outline   Minton Green ~ Callow Hollow ~ The Portway ~ Minton Hill ~ Packetstone Hill ~ Minton Green.

Summary   The route starts in the little Saxon village of Minton and then follows the stream in one of the Long Mynd valleys to the summit. It continues along the ancient Bronze Age track known as the Portway and descends on good tracks down Minton and Packetstone Hills.

Attractions   It is like going back in time seeing the quiet Saxon hamlet of Minton with its cottages clustered round the green. There is a fine example of a cruck-framed house and a moated Saxon mound and in early Spring the little green is covered in daffodils. The name Minton is from the Old English and means 'the settlement on the hill'.

Callow Hollow is a wild and beautiful Long Mynd valley and it is haven for many birds. The family might surprise a heron fishing and in Summer look out for the ring ouzel — the mountain blackbird. Wheatears, stonechats and whinchats nest in the heather-covered hills. It is exciting to wade the shallow streams and to watch the antics of the dipper bobbing and diving in the water. Children will love the miniature Oakleymill waterfall and in Summer foxgloves grow thickly in Callow Coppice.

Along the crest of the Long Mynd runs an ancient trackway called the Portway first used by Stone Age traders and later by cattle drovers. The summit is also the headquarters of the Midland Gliding Club and the family will enjoy watching the gliders soaring over the heather. This is an ideal place for gliding because the prevailing south west wind blowing against the west facing escarpment provides excellent up-currents. Look out for hanggliders too. Buzzards fly high over the Long Mynd gliding on the thermals and the gliders seem to imitate their flight.

The well-rutted track leading steeply up behind the village of Minton was once a packhorse route over the hill to Bishops Castle. There is a rocky outcrop on Packetstone Hill and the drover would stand on the rock to adjust the load on the ponies before the descent to Minton.

Refreshments   Little Stretton, Green Dragon, Ragleth Arms. See Route 13.

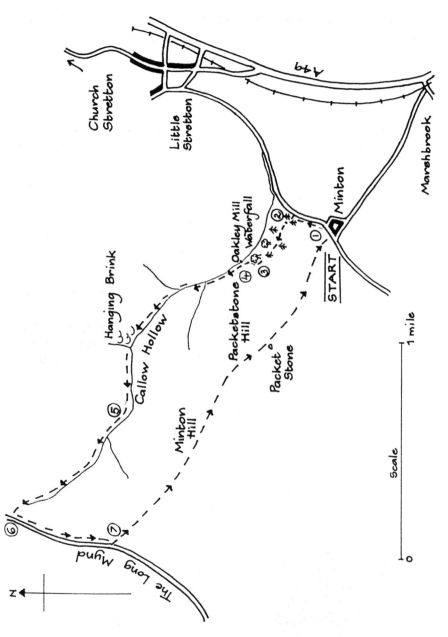

64

Route 14

Minton Green and Callow Hollow   4½ miles

START   *Minton Green. At Marshbrook on the A49 between Craven Arms and Church Stretton a minor road leads to Minton and there is plenty of parking around the Green. GR 432908.*

ROUTE

1. *Take the lane towards Little Stretton. At the bottom of the steep slope turn left through a gap in the hedge into a small conifer plantation.*

2. *After 10 yards turn right into the trees by a wooden waymark post marked Callow Hollow.*

3. *Turn left at the fence and follow the narrow path up to a stile and into the Hollow joining the stream on your right.*

4. *Follow the stream passing Oakleymill waterfall. Continue up the valley which widens slightly to an outcrop of rock called Hanging Brink.*

5. *As the stream becomes narrower bear right passing a pool on your left and continue in the same direction until you reach a metalled road.*

6. *Turn left along the road until you reach a wooden marker post on your left marked 'Minton'.*

7. *Turn left onto a wide track and follow this down to the hamlet. The track becomes steeper until you reach a gate and the National Trust sign for Minton. Pass through the gate and follow the track through barns and cottages to reach Minton Green.*

ACCESS BY BUS

To Marshbrook from Church Stretton and Ludlow.

SMALL COPPER

WILDERHOPE MANOR

Route 15   3½ miles

Wilderhope Manor

Outline   Wilderhope Manor ~ Stanway Coppice ~ Lower Stanway ~ Wilderhope.

Summary   This walk starts from the Elizabethan manor house of Wilderhope which stands in a remote and beautiful valley. It climbs up to the wooded ridge of Stanway Coppice with wonderful views over Wenlock Edge to the Long Mynd and the return route follows the stream through the valley on part of the Shropshire Way. Wilderhope is owned by the National Trust and used as a Youth Hostel and the house is open to the public on Saturday afternoons 2–4.30 p.m. and also on Wednesday afternoons in Summer.

Attractions   Wilderhope is an interesting manor house for the family to explore. It is remarkable that it has survived unaltered, looking very much as it was originally built in the 16th century. The house is built of the local Aymestry limestone but the tall chimney stacks are of intricate brickwork. An unusual feature is the main spiral staircase which leads from the ground floor to the attics capped with a conical roof. Each step is made from a solid block of oak.

There is an exciting story connected with the house. Thomas Smallwood of Wilderhope Manor was a Major in the Royalist army during the Civil War. On one occasion when he was carrying important secret despatches for the King he was captured by a party of Cromwell's troops and taken to his own house at Wilderhope. He was imprisoned in an upper room but he escaped by a secret exit, ran to the stable and fled on his horse. The soldiers caught up with him at the spot where the Plough Inn stands today and the Major seeing that escape was impossible rode his horse over Wenlock Edge. His fall was broken by a crab apple tree and although his horse was killed he escaped and delivered his despatches to Shrewsbury. The limestone crag is still known as the Major's Leap.

Wenlock Edge is a distinctive part of the Shropshire hills. From the west it appears a long escarpment and yet from the east it is only a gentle swell. Its shape and vegetation are due to the beds of limestone rock which lie underneath. The Wenlock Limestone was formed 420 million years ago in a tropical sea — it was built up largely from the skeletons and shells of sea creatures. Earth movements have tilted the rock strata and this dip is responsible for the shape of the Edge.

continued on page 70

Route 15

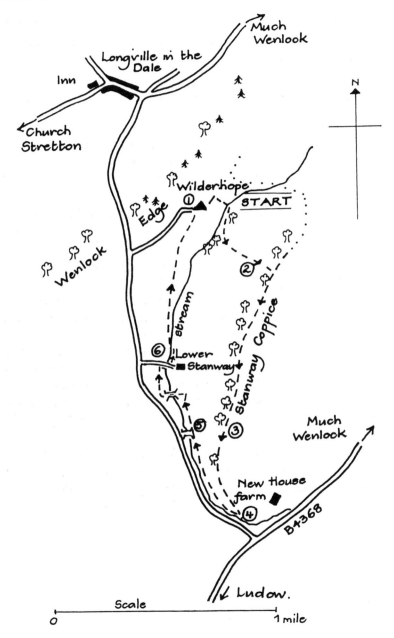

Much Wenlook

Longville in the Dale

Inn

Church Stretton

N

Wilderhope

① START

Edge

Wenlock

②

Stanway Coppice

stream

⑥ Lower Stanway

⑤

③

Much Wenlook

New House Farm

④

B4368

Ludow.

Scale

0   1 mile

68

Route 15

Wilderhope Manor   3½ miles

START *Wilderhope Manor on the minor road between Longville in the Dale and Munslow. There is a small car park at the house.*

ROUTE

1. *Take the track behind Wilderhope Manor, go past the Field Studies house on the left and through a gate marked with the Shropshire Way buzzard. Turn right immediately and walk down the track to the stile. The marker post says Stanway Coppice. Cross another stile and follow the track to the right. It crosses a shallow ford and curves round through the woods climbing slightly. Follow the marker posts across a field to a stream passing a large pool.*

2. *Walk straight up the field to the stile. Turn right and climb upwards through woodland of beeches and oaks. Pass a marker post to Wilderhope and continue along the Ridge.*

3. *The track emerges in a field. Turn right and follow the fence down to New House farm passing through 4 fields.*

4. *Just before New House farm turn right and cross over a stile near a large footbridge and some cottages. Turn right and follow the stream to Lower Stanway.*

5. *Pass an old stone bridge and cross a stile. Cross a second stile and follow a waymarked detour to the left of the farm. This crosses to a marker post in the field then goes left to a stone bridge and a stile with a buzzard sign. Continue across a field to a fence and on to a stile on the farm drive. Turn right, walk over the bridge and cross the stile on the left.*

6. *The route follows the stream on the left for a short distance and then crosses a footbridge on the left and a stile with the buzzard sign. The stream is now on the right, pass a large pool and continue along the valley to Wilderhope which will soon come in sight.*

Limestone areas are rich in flowering plants. Look out for yellow wort with its stalk of yellow flowers, cowslips in early summer and later in the year straw-coloured Carline thistles. In September large Red Admiral butterflies flutter on the plants in Stanway Coppice. Perhaps the children might see a small Copper butterfly — its wings gleaming in the sun.

Refreshments Longville Arms. Children welcome, picnic tables.

HEATH CHAPEL

Nordy Bank on Brown Clee

Outline The Yeld ~ Nordy Bank ~ The Yeld.

Summary This walk is always a great favourite with young children. It is short and exciting and on wide grassy tracks which are easy to follow. The walk starts near the little village of Stoke St. Milborough and climbs up to the ancient hill fort of Nordy Bank. The ramparts are a wonderful place for hide and seek and picnics. From the hill fort children can see a real panorama including their path home across the Yeld.

Attractions The Clee Hills are one of the most striking landscapes in Shropshire. Brown Clee at nearly 1,800 feet is the highest in the county but Titterstone Clee with its shining radar dome is more distinctive in shape and seems higher. The children will be able to spot this landmark from other Shropshire hills — on a clear day you can see the dome from the Long Mynd — 12 miles away. Tradition says that Titterstone's name came from a large rocking stone on the hill called the 'totterstone'. Since the 13th century minerals have been extracted from the hills — coal, copper, limestone, iron ore and dhustone — a very hard rock which is excellent road stone.

     The hills encouraged a great number of legends and superstitions. It was for example considered unlucky to put a baby in a cradle before it had been christened. A girl looking for a husband would place a ladybird on her finger and toss it into the air as she chanted.

     Ladybird, ladybird fly away flee.

     Tell me which way my wedding's to be

     Uphill or downhill or towards the Brown Clee.

Her husband would come from the direction in which the insect flew.

     Only quarrying for roadstone goes on today on Titterstone Clee and the relics of past industries merge with the small farms. There are several hill forts on the hills but sadly they have been destroyed by industrial activity. Nordy Bank on Brown Clee remains intact and this is an ideal walk to introduce the family to the Clee Hills.

     Can the children spy the radio masts on Clee Burf and Abdon Burf and the Long Mynd on the horizon? The Commoners still graze sheep and horses on the hills and if your visit is in August you may be lucky enough to see the annual round up. There are foxes on Brown Clee and sometimes the scarlet coats of Ludlow hunt. Watch out for meadow pipits and yellowhammers and cock pheasants.

continued on page 73

71

Route 16

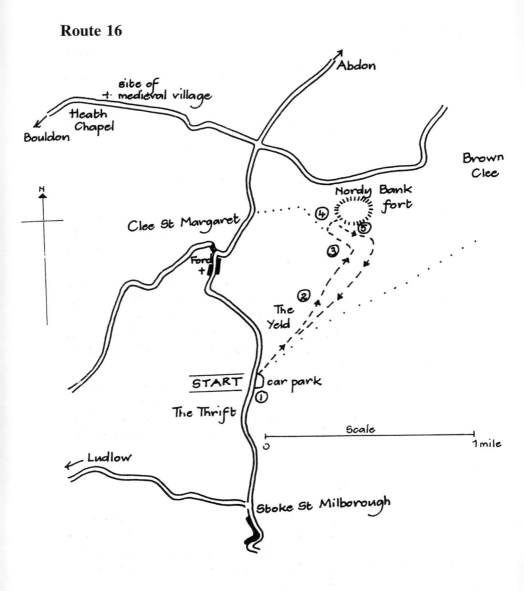

Route 16

Nordy Bank on Brown Clee   3 miles

START *There is a little parking area at the Yeld on the minor road between Stoke St. Milborough and Abdon.*

ROUTE

1. *Climb the stile and walk along the broad grassy track of the Yeld keeping near the left hand fence and passing a gabled cottage.*

2. *Where the fence curves left veer right slightly uphill. Another fence joins on the left and the track follows the fence again and passes 2 cottages.*

3. *The track turns sharply to the left, Nordy Bank is above on the right. Where the fence curves round follow the higher track and after 100 yards take the grassy ride on the right and begin the gentle climb to the ramparts.*

4. *Cross the track circling the fort and take the track opposite climbing to the right. Walk round the ramparts to the first opening. This is the spot where the return journey starts. After exploring the fort stand on the ramparts and look towards Titterstone Clee. You can see a high track through the bracken heading towards a wooded enclosure on the horizon — this is your path home.*

5. *Walk down to a wide ride, turn left and then shortly afterwards take the right track. Follow this path as it climbs upwards and pass to the right of a large hawthorn tree. Where the path divides take the right fork and walk across the Yeld alongside the higher fence back to the parking place.*

ACCESS BY BUS
To Stoke St. Milborough from Ludlow.

There is an air of mystery and magic surrounding Nordy Bank. The children will enjoy exploring the ramparts — they can walk round the perimeter of the fort and it's a wonderful place for games and a picnic. Do read the children's book Nordy Bank by Sheena Porter, about a family who camp on the Iron Age fort.

Before your return home perhaps the family would enjoy seeing the long ford at Clee St. Margaret or visiting Heath Chapel a tiny Norman church standing in a lonely field. Heath is also the site of an abandoned medieval village – can the children guess why this happened?

Refreshments Tally Ho Inn, Bouldon. Garden.

Appendices

ROUTES IN ORDER OF DIFFICULTY

Easy short walks
 Route 1 — *Ludlow Castle and the River Teme — 2¼ miles*
 Route 2 — *Mary Knoll Forest Trail — 3½ miles*
 Route 3 — *Croft Castle and Fishpool Valley — 3½ miles*
 Route 8 — *Bury Ditches — 1½ miles*
 Route 16 — *Nordy Bank — 3 miles*

Longer walks
 Route 4 — *Offa's Dyke and the Monument — 4 miles*
 Route 6 — *Stokesay Castle and View Edge — 4½ miles*
 Route 10 — *Mitchell's Fold — 4½ miles*
 Route 14 — *Minton Green and Callow Hollow — 4½ miles*
 Route 15 — *Wilderhope Manor — 3½ miles*

Strenuous walks
 Route 5 — *Offa's Dyke and Panpunton Hill — 5 miles*
 Route 7 — *The Arbor Tree — 7 miles*
 Route 9 — *Kerry Ridgeway and the Cantlin Stone — 6 miles*
 Route 11 — *The Stiperstones and the Devil's Chair — 6 miles*
 Route 13 — *Ashes Hollow and Pole Bank — 5½ miles*

BUS AND RAIL TIMETABLES

Shropshire County Council produce a comprehensive Bus and Train Map and Guide which is available at Tourist Information Centres and Travel Centres.

Telephone Enquiries. The County Council also have an Enquiry Service for countywide information on bus, express coach and train services. Telephone 0345-056785.
Monday to Friday 8.30 a.m.–5.45 p.m.
Saturday 8.30 a.m.–5 p.m.
County Council sponsored Travel Centres have been opened in Oswestry, Shrewsbury and Telford to give information on all services and to help you plan your journey.

Timetables. The Shropshire Bus Guide contains timetables for all local bus services and may be consulted at Shropshire Libraries. Timetable leaflets are also available from libraries and Information Centres.

SHROPSHIRE EXPLORER'S KIT

Scenesetters at Church Stretton produce a Shropshire Explorer's kit for a small payment to cover handling and postage. This includes the Shropshire Bus & Train Map and Guide, the Shropshire Wayfarer Leaflet, Guide to quiet country places, lists for walks, trails and maps, booklist and information on activities and events.
Scenesetters, Bircher Cottage, Little Stretton, Church Stretton, Shropshire SY6 6RE.

YOUTH HOSTELS

Youth Hostels cater for families now and children love the fun and freedom of a YHA holiday. Many hostels have family rooms and self catering facilities are very helpful for family mealtimes. If you want to explore a new area with the family try one or two nights at a Youth Hostel — it solves the problem of long expeditions and car journeys and gives parents a welcome break too. There are 6 Youth Hostels in this area in beautiful countryside.

Bridges. Hugh Gibbins Memorial Hostel. Tel. Linley 656. Routes 11, 12.
Clun. The Mill. Tel. Craven Arms 582. Routes 7, 8, 9.
Knighton. Old Primary School. Tel. Knighton 528807. Routes 4, 5.
Ludlow. Ludford Lodge. Tel. Ludlow 2472. Routes 1, 2.
Wheathill. Malthouse Farm. Tel. Burwarton 236. Route 16.
Wilderhope Manor. Tel. Longville 363. Routes 6, 13, 14, 15.

WET WEATHER ALTERNATIVES. COMPLETELY OR PARTLY UNDER COVER

Museums

Aston Munslow. White House Museum of Buildings and Country Life. April to October.
Bridgnorth Museum, Northgate. April to end September.
Postern Gate, Museum of Childhood and Costumes. Open all year.
Clun Town Trust Museum. Easter to end October.
Cosford Aerospace Museum. Open all year, except weekends December to February.
Ironbridge Gorge Museum. On several sites, most open all year: Coalbrookdale Museum of Iron, Jackfield Tile Museum, Blists Hill Open Air Museum, The Tar Tunnel, Bedlam Furnaces and the Iron Bridge itself.
Ludlow Museum, Butter Cross. Collection of fossils, arms and armour. Mid-March to end September except Sundays.
Midland Motor Museum, Stanmore. Open all year.
Much Wenlock Museum. April to September except Sunday.

HISTORIC BUILDINGS OPEN TO THE PUBLIC

Berrington Hall (National Trust), near Leominster. Shop, tea-room. Open May-September.
Buildwas Abbey, near Ironbridge. Substantial remains of Norman abbey of about 1200.
Clun Castle. Remains of Norman Castle, may be seen at any time, no charge.
Croft Castle (National Trust), near Leominster. Open May-September.
Dudmaston Hall (National Trust), near Bridgnorth. A 17th century house with collections of furniture and Dutch flower paintings.
Eardington, Daniels Mill, near Bridgnorth. Largest working water-wheel in Britain. Saturday and Sunday from Easter to end of September.
Heath Chapel. An almost unaltered Norman church. It stands alone on the site of a deserted village.
Ludlow Castle. Shropshire's largest castle. Open 7 days a week from May to September 10.30 a.m.–6 p.m. October to April it is open from 10.30 a.m.–4 p.m. and closed Sundays.

Much Wenlock, The Priory. A Norman monastery on an ancient Anglo-Saxon site.
Shipton Hall. An Elizabethan mansion with a dovecote and a secret tunnel. Open May
to September.
Stokesay Castle. Fortified manor house (English Heritage). Open daily except
Tuesdays. Summer 10 a.m.–6 p.m., Winter 10 a.m.–4.30 p.m.
Wilderhope Manor, near Easthope (National Trust), 16th century stone mansion in a
secluded valley. Now a Youth Hostel.

PRIVATE RAILWAYS

Bridgnorth Castle Hill Railway. A two-car funicular railway between High Town and
Low Town, closed Christmas Day and Boxing Day.
Severn Valley Railway. Steam trains run between Bridgnorth and Kidderminster,
weekends March to October and daily mid-May to early September.

WILDLIFE

Acton Scott Working Farm Museum. End March to end October. Tel. Marshbrook
306/307.
The Wernlas Collection. A living museum of rare breeds of poultry. Onibury, near
Ludlow. Open daily Easter-October. Closed Mondays except Bank Holidays. Tel.
Bromfield 318.

OUTDOOR SHOWS AND FESTIVALS

Arbor Day, Aston on Clun. May 29th.
Bishops Castle Traction Engine Rally. August Bank Holiday. Tel. Baschurch 260595.
Burwarton Show. First Thursday in August. Tel. Stoke St. Milborough 309.
Cosford Air Day. A Sunday in June. Tel. Albrighton 4872.
Cheney Longville, Craven Arms. Shropshire Game Fair, first weekend after the May
bank holiday. Tel. Craven Arms 2708.
Cruckton. Horse and Tractor Ploughing Championship of the British Isles. Last
Saturday in September. Tel. Church Stretton 722701.
Ludlow Festival. Last week in June, first week in July.
Shrewsbury Flower Show. Middle of August. Tel. Shrewsbury 64051.

SWIMMING POOLS AND LEISURE CENTRES

Bridgnorth Sports and Leisure Centre, Northgate.
Cleobury Mortimer, Lacon Childe Sports Centre.
Ludlow Swimming Pool, Dinham Bridge.
Much Wenlock Sports Centre, Farley Road.
Much Wenlock Outdoor Swimming Pool.
Tenbury Wells Swimming Pool.
Telford Ice Rink, Telford Town Centre.

TOURIST INFORMATION CENTRES

Bridgnorth. The Library, Listley Street. Tel. 3358.
Church Stretton. The Library, Church Street. Tel. 722535.
Ironbridge Museum. Visitor Centre. Tel. 2166.
Knighton. Information Centre, The Old School. Tel. 528753.
Ludlow. Information Centre, Castle Street. Tel. 3857.
Leominster. Information Centre, 6 School Lane. Tel. 6460.
Presteigne. Information Centre, Old Market Hall. Tel. 260193.

FURTHER READING

Shropshire Hill Country — Vincent Waite (J. M. Dent).
The Shropshire Landscape — Trevor Rowley (Hodder and Stoughton).
Shropshire Hills — H. W. Timperley (J. M. Dent).
A light-hearted look at our Shropshire history — Jean Hughes (Wilding).
A History of Shropshire — Barrie Trinder.
Shropshire Gazetteer — Michael Raven.
Shropshire and Herefordshire Villages — George H. Haines (Robert Hale).
Walking Ancient Trackways — Michael Dunn (David and Charles).
Exploring the Marches and Borderlands of Wales — W. T. Barber.
Shropshire — Brian Bailey (Hale).
Shropshire — Shropshire County Council.

THE MEDIEVAL BRIDGE, CLUN

The Family Walks Series

Family Walks on Anglesey. Laurence Main ISBN 0 907758 665.

Family Walks in Berkshire & North Hampshire. Kathy Sharp ISBN 0 907758 371.

Family Walks around Bristol, Bath & the Mendips. Nigel Vile ISBN 0 907758 193.

Family Walks around Cardiff & the Valleys. Gordon Hindess ISBN 0 907758 541.

Family Walks in Cheshire. Chris Buckland ISBN 0 907758 290.

Family Walks in Cornwall. John Caswell. ISBN 0 907758 55X.

Family Walks in the Cotswolds. Gordon Ottewell ISBN 0 907758 150.

Family Walks on Exmoor & the Quantocks. John Caswell ISBN 0 907758 460.

Family Walks in South Gloucestershire. Gordon Ottewell ISBN 0 907758 339.

Family Walks in Gower. Amanda Green ISBN 0 907758 630.

Family Walks in Hereford and Worcester. Gordon Ottewell ISBN 0 907758 207.

Family Walks on the Isle of Wight. Laurence Main ISBN 0 907758 568.

Family Walks in North West Kent. Clive Cutter ISBN 0 907758 363.

Family Walks in the Lake District. Barry McKay ISBN 0 907758 401.

Family Walks in Mendip, Avalon & Sedgemoor. Nigel Vile ISBN 0 907758 41X.

Family Walks in the New Forest. Nigel Vile ISBN 0 907758 606.

Family Walks in Oxfordshire. Laurence Main ISBN 0 907758 38X.

Family Walks in the Dark Peak. Norman Taylor ISBN 0 907758 169.

Family Walks in the White Peak. Norman Taylor ISBN 0 907758 096.

Family Walks in South Derbyshire. Gordon Ottewell ISBN 0 907758 614.

Family Walks in South Shropshire. Marian Newton ISBN 0 907758 304.

Family Walks in Snowdonia. Laurence Main ISBN 0 907758 320.

Family Walks in the Staffordshire Peaks and Potteries. Les Lumsdon ISBN 0 907758 347.

Family Walks around Stratford & Banbury. Gordon Ottewell ISBN 0 907758 495.

Family Walks in Suffolk. C. J. Francis ISBN 0 907758 649.

Family Walks around Swansea. Raymond Humphreys ISBN 0 907758 622.

Family Walks in the Teme Valley. Camilla Harrison ISBN 0 907758 452.

Family Walks in Three Peaks & Malham. Howard Beck ISBN 0 907758 428.

Family Walks in Mid Wales. Laurence Main ISBN 0 907758 274.

Family Walks in the North Wales Borderlands. Gordon Emery ISBN 0 907758 509.

Family Walks in Warwickshire. Geoff Allen ISBN 0 907758 533.

Family Walks in the Weald of Kent & Sussex. Clive Cutter ISBN 0 907758 517.

Family Walks in Wiltshire. Nigel Vile ISBN 0 907758 215.

Family Walks in the Wye Valley. Heather & Jon Hurley ISBN 0 907758 266.

Family Walks in the North Yorkshire Dales. Howard Beck ISBN 0 907758 525.

Family Walks in South Yorkshire. Norman Taylor ISBN 0 907758 258.

Family Walks in West Yorkshire. Howard Beck ISBN 0 907758 436.

The publishers welcome suggestions for further titles in this series; and will be pleased to consider manuscripts relating to Derbyshire from new or established authors.

Scarthin Books of Cromford, in the Peak District, are also leading second-hand and antiquarian booksellers, and are eager to purchase specialised material, both ancient and modern.
Contact Dr D. J. Mitchell, 0629-823272.